Cassie Premo Steele imagines worlds that are luminous, magical, and filled with a beauty only she can capture in writing. She gifts us these worlds with words that fly off the page, transporting us to a realm where spirit soars freely. Here, we are transformed by beauty, grief, and joy – a well that renews and restores us for the work of love we are all meant to do.

—Barbara Boswell,
South African novelist and author of *Grace*

"Poetry, which dimly fades on wood,/ smells of heat and violence,/ tears the mask from silence,/ lone survivor,/ canoe that floats eternally," writes Cassie Premo Steele in her poem, "Bunk Bed in the Holocaust Museum." This aptly captures the unique understanding of her art that defines Steele as one of our prominent voices in today's literary arena. Her new poetry collection, *Tongues in Trees* (Unbound Content, 2017) proffers us a buffet of her heartfelt, profound, insightful poetry spanning more than two decades of opening our eyes and hearts to the silent and spoken griefs, the big and small losses, the healed and bleeding hurts, the evanescent and pinpointed joys of women real and mythical: sisters, mothers, concentration camp survivors, witches, terminal patients, abused children, poets—all memorable, poignant fellow beings representing the panoply of humanity.

—Thelma T. Reyna
Award-Winning Poet, Former Poet Laureate
Rising, Falling, All of Us (Golden Foothills Press, 2014)

Cassie Premo Steele no tiene pelos en la lenga! In my country of origin, Puerto Rico, this dicho has a meaning which is complimentary if you're fearless in speaking truth or more than a bit disparaging if you're not. This book, aptly titled *Tongues in Trees*, is a compilation of Cassie Premo Steele's work reflecting 23 years of her beautiful and powerful words in poetry form that stick in my mind for the truth they tell, for the way she's able to convey "from the kiskas" (Yiddish term meanings guts) the truth she's lived and inhabited since a child. Through her poems she recounts stories of her early childhood, some very dark, and later ones deriving from her time spent in a Spanish-speaking country that only widened her wisdom and her outlook on the world, on love, on social issues and, yes, even politics. But there are poesy stories on her daughter, on loves and lovers, stories garnered through observations both simple and complex, some painful, many joyful brimming with sanguinity. This book was in fact, a joy to read, even the "sad parts" in retrospect...and I look forward to reading it again and again, each time no doubt I'll find new succulent parts to savor.

—Lydia Cortés
Whose Place

There are questions our souls keenly wish we would ask. These poems both pose and answer them. These poems are filled with that which is inexplicable yet gasp-eliciting, delicate yet steely, crushed yet abloom. Their echoes, slyness, rhythms, and rhymes anchor this poet in the company of Susan Howe, Emily Dickinson, and Christina Rossetti. These poems open up to the reader like a heart.

—Candace Walsh
Licking the Spoon: A Memoir of Food, Family, and Identity

The way Cassie Premo Steele marries words together produces a myriad of emotions in readers. Whether it's delight, consternation, joy, anger, or awe, her words provide a refuge in a world in need of this kind of beautiful poetry that shines a healing light on the world's shadows. Use this collection of poems as your mental and spiritual first-aid kit and break it open often when the world seems too much to bear.

—Candace Chellew-Hodge
*Bulletproof Faith: A Spiritual Survival Guide
for Gay and Lesbian Christians*

tongues in trees

poems 1994-2017

tongues in trees
poems 1994-2017

cassie
premo
steele

ISBN 978-1-936373-56-7
Published in the United States
by Unbound Content, LLC, Englewood, NJ.
Cover design: ©2017 Susanne Kappler
Book design: ©2017 Dana Martin
The poems in this collection are all original and previously unpublished with the exception of those listed in the credits page at the end of the volume.

TONGUES IN TREES
First edition 2017

UNBOUND
CONTENT

for Annmarie,
who believed

Contents

1994-2004

2006-2016

2017

And this, our life, exempt from public haunt, finds tongues in trees, books in the running brooks, sermons in stones, and good in everything.

William Shakespeare

1994

2004

Well

well,
here we are
swapping secrets
like jewels
in foggy alleyways
shiny currency
buys the knowing
well
going deeper
to the water
flowing
currents below
frozen ground
quenching thirst so
well
done daily
like prayer
we press our lips
against the words
gently
giving
well.

Antidote for Witches

for Anne Sexton

The antidote for witches
Is to take inside your mouth
The sounding of their voices
And slowly spit them out.

So let their songs be seeds and soil
And your own voice be the sun
Smoothly strongly saying
What you wish be done.

For mouths make miracles and many
From crazy and alone
And take magic from together
Uncovering more than one.

Laura's Song

He carries you up high
I walk beside below
You call my name and sing
A song for me alone:

"If, if I was a witch
I was a good witch good"
Not were but was, I think:
I was a witch, and good?

"And ride a horse in sand"
A horse in sand, you sing
I dreamt a witch, on horse
You sing some more, I think:

Was I your age, at three?
Which witch was I, at five?
Was I a witch, or she?
Where was that horse, at night?

Or did she come on horse
To frighten me below?
Like you on him, so high
And me below, so low.

Guadalupe

I came
far from my home
to you

I wanted
a continent
with a different tongue

and there
I found
you

most days you watched me
talk
while you listened

I did not know
what people call you
in your real life

for weeks I called you another name
and on the last day
you told me

your family
and the people who love you
call you Lupe

for Guadalupe
is your middle name,
the name in your middle

and even then I could not say it
it was as if suddenly you revealed
what you wanted me to know

and I was caught
I thought I knew you
already

in my mind
your body is a dark mountain
rising below the cool sky

and my finger comes
from above to touch
you

Guadalupe
in the middle
and it makes

a river
water gushing through the center
as I say your name

the name you taught me
not the one I thought I knew
Guadalupe

you are
not the one
I thought I knew.

Guadalupe

Yo fui
lejos de mi hogar
a ti

yo quisé
un continente
con una lengua differente

y allí
yo te
encontré

muchos días tu me mirabas
hablar
a la vez que tu escuchabas

yo no sabía
que la gente te llama
en tu vida real

por semanas yo te llamaba otro nombre
y el último día
tu me dijiste

que tu família
y la gente que te ama
te llaman Lupe

por que Guadalupe
es tu nombre mitad,
el nombre en tu mitad

y aun entonces yo no podía decirlo
era como si tu revelabas de súbito
lo que tú me querías supiera

y yo estaba atrapada
yo pensaba que te conocía
ya

en mi mente
tu cuerpo es una montaña oscura
subiendo debajo del cielo fresco

y mi dedo viene
desde arriba para tocarte
a ti

Guadalupe
en el mitad
y esto hace

un rio
agua borbollando por el centro
cuando yo digo tu nombre

el nombre que tú me enseñaste
no lo que yo pensaba que yo conocía
Guadalupe

tu eres
no lo que
yo pensaba que conocía.

In the House of the Sun

In the house of the sun there is
A yellow just for you; it shines
Even brighter when you are
Not looking or waiting.
In the house of the moon there is
A white just for you; it holds
Your worries, your fears, your wants;
It rocks them all to sleep.
In the house of your heart there are
So many colors we cannot count
Or name them; they swirl together
Endlessly healing, healing, healing.

You write what you cannot say

You wait, in those moments of silence,
to be able to be alone with the pen.
You look, after someone asks you
the impossible, at your hands, and you wait.

It was an edict, attached to you
at birth like the slip of paper inside
a fortune cookie. It was a male god
who gave you this promise, this pledge.

For years you traced your fingers
along the edge of the pew in front
of you, writing all you could not
say, while the priest went on and on.

You do not go to church anymore,
but on Sundays and other quiet
days, you still sit tracing with
your fingers on thighs and lips and eyes.

Even now, after faith has returned to you
in the form of a woman, you know
that god is also in some measure a man
who gave you this curse, this blessing, this plan.

To Have Been Left

Witchcraft originates in carnal lust, which in women is insatiable.
Pope Innocent VIII, <u>Malleus Maleficarum</u>

I must confess I miss my witch –
the flowing way she'd come
in silent, biding, me alone.

My own voices speak clearer now
– or softer anyhow –
they whisper, gentle – prayers.

It is lonely, though, to have been left,
and strange, now, to be right,
and be the only one who knows.

Healing

Scar tissue
You can say that again
You can say it
You can say
You can

Scars
I don't want to hear it
I don't want to hear about it
I don't want to hear any more about it

Scar tissue attaches itself
Needs to be cut
Needs to bleed
Needs to heal again

Scars need to heal separately
Need to be separate
I need to be separate
I am a separate person
I am not attached

Pain
Pain changes things
Changes come
Change will come

And go
Let it go
Let myself go
Let go
Go myself

Come two women

Come two women
through the forest
dark hair and eyes
bright with the glow
from the sun in
their spirits know
of laughter and
soul kisses which
touch hands and this
is life and this
is death and all
is good.
                    Evil
is forgetting
sunlight spirits
and kisses.

Be good and do
not forget, the
women whisper
as they walk away.

Tending

I feel me stiffen to the pain
of buried memory
and pretending
will not make it go away:
as I float above the bed
looking down,
pretending
I don't exist.
I'm 'tending 'tending 'tending,
tending to the long forgotten
smallest part of me
whose voice threatens
to open like a cavern
unfolding her throat
and exposing her bowels
swallowing me up
until I don't exist
for real.
The fear keeps me steady
and I'm tending
fires in my belly
burning long and slow
making me remember
making me the tender.

Witches at My Party

I can tell
From the smell
Of gas
From the kitchen,

And the fear
That clasps
My back
With paws

There will
Be witches
At my party
Tonight.

Last night
My father
Raped me
In a dream

And I was glad
When it was over
As when looking
Through a windshield

You realize
You survived
The accident
But still wonder if you're dead.

With these questions
I will greet the guests:
Good and bad,
Silent and cackling,

They move
Into me
And I
Wonder

Who
Will have
A body
To hold me from without?

Your voice, father

Your voice, father, has been banished
from my head since I was two. You
were walking away from us, as
I watched through the dusty
window pane, and from behind
me came another voice, my mother:
He's going to the shrink. And you
did. You did shrink, first from
my heart as it skittered
away each time you
touched me. Your voice,
coming in for a kiss, your
pleading, watery voice
I shrunk from. You
retreated for the final but not
the last time when your voice
halted, on that day you
left, and your tears
took the place of your voice.
After all the years
I could not stand your voice,
its absence was worse, as
I stared at your eyes
filling with tears and
I thought: He is not even a man
enough to go bravely. Your voice,
from far away, interrupted
my life at punctures after that,
half angry, half sad,
asking after the woman
I was becoming, and later,
after the woman
I'd become. Your voice,

I banished for the last time
at twenty-two, and then,
silent, as if through that
dusty window pane again, you
returned, this time in
my dreams. Your voice,
knowing I would not hear it,
became vivid colors, the yellow
and purple fish speaking to
me, the black gun shooting
me, the sounds of fish and guns,
but not your voice. Your voice,
father, had been banished from
my head since I was two.

America, my mother

America, my mother, why is it so hard to be
a family.

America
my father

read Allen Ginsberg in the seminary,
then he broke out,
pierced my mother twice, to make us.
It occurs to me that I am America, he said,
once in fumbling,
once in rage.

America
my brother

lost somewhere, riding Carolina,
a redneck in a sportscar,
drinking like his father,
who married my mother, who says,
It's nobody's fault
but your own.

America
my son

I would have called you Corey,
from the core of me,
they cut you out of me.
After the priest, first laughing, then said,
he could not absolve me
of me.

America
my daughter

all this wishing will never make you a boy.
It is fun to be a girl, I say,
trying to make you see
how pretty I am. See how pretty, I say,
making you look
in the mirror.

America, my mother, why is it so hard to be
a family.

Asherah

In the midst of this flat field
my master owns a house
where I sit on the porch and milk
babies.

I am the mother to all the light
children, who grow bigger
than my breast and forget
my name.

One night in my cabin I heard
a bird sing to the moon,
and I knew then that I was a
woman.

When he beat me the next time
I saw in the ground a spider
spinning where my body had crushed
her web.

I had no choice but to follow
the bird when he called me.

To the east he flew, to the moon,
and then later, more tired, to the sun.

In the morning I saw the sea
and I knew from the whispered
stories of women that it was
my home.

Not the sea itself, but her other
shore, where the edge opened into
a blanket of ferns at the base of a
forest.

I entered, as the sun climbed higher,
and saw the future:
sun, house, man, land.

Like a child's schoolbook, each word
above me, a world to come for centuries.

The sea took me into her.
The bird sang my name.
I heard babies crying.

When I reached bottom, it was cool
and the sun could no longer
touch me.

Field Trip to the Art Museum

In America our children live with memories.

Two young black boys watch a painting
Hanging on a white wall in a Southern city
Where the Confederate flag waves on the Capitol.
They shift their feet with nervous energy
And say, "Those kids are tugging at their momma
Cause they're hungry and she's mad."

Back at the shelter their mother sucks hard
On one cigarette after another and thinks
About showering off the fast food smell
Of her day at work. It's Friday night
And she wishes for a Grandmother in the country
To take the boys for the weekend
So she can go dancing in a silky dress
And sleep until noon the next day.

"But she's gonna give them some bread,"
The boys say, still standing at the wall.
On the way back to the shelter, they pass
A donut shop and say, "Once we went
To a donut shop. They got all kinds and
You can get chocolate if you want and
They got coffee for the adults and the kids
Can get water." It's almost supper-time.

In America our children live with memories.

Pandora

I am birch bark, white on one side,
sprinkled with soft lines
where traces of paths are worn thin.

I am cotton, shooting from brown pods
that open like stars that reverse, dark suns,
bright nights, when dying.

I am a gray pod, fallen from the tree,
shut in upon myself, but filled
with tiny seeds that lie drying.

I am a stone, light as a tooth,
with soft curves where waves have washed,
and left their hands upon me.

I am a snail shell, curled like a clock,
circles opening ever wider, making believe
that any path could be so easy.

I am a lump from the ground,
striped like a tiger or a highway,
laced with chalk and skin from history.

I am a root, wrinkled with age,
filled with the smell of frankincense
and where your fingernails press, I bleed.

I am a tree branch, covered with lichen,
peeled in soft places and clinging to hope,
I show what pulses underneath.

Kore

I start the day with music in my room at home.
I have no other lover, mother, than myself alone.

I leave the house of elders, start running to my life.
My body, quick and hungry, my mind, a waiting knife.

I see the older women watch my legs as I run.
Their eyes hit my skin with wild envy. I am so young.

In the world, I use my heart and feel no fear.
It beats faster when what I love comes near.

Colors and voices feed me instead of food.
When I walk I love to watch my bones move.

I am almost a boy I am so thin.
When I kiss one, I kiss my own skin.

I do not yet hate boys like women.
They have not hurt me like men.

In my world of music, color, shape and skin,
I still forget what later will remember. Until then

I am my body, filled with wheat and foam.
Days I dance, nights I sleep alone.

Even other bodies in my bed, I am alone.
I have learned to love the daybreak.

I can run outside again.
I will not always be so lonesome in my stride.

The day will come, and I will trust it.
I will run to it like I have before.

Before I reach the sun they will stop me.
There will be women who will hate me.

There will be men who will know me.
There will be boys who will beat me.

In the middle of the circle, I will search.
For the first time, I will want another girl.

I will not see her there.
They will enclose me, men and boys and women.

They will dance me into the ground.
I will go under. I will come back up.

I will bring other girls with me.

Ishtar

What happened to the wildflowers
I remember planting long ago?
What action caused such scorn
That they refuse to grow?
Have I been gone so long
To miss the season's flow?

Underground there is a desert.
They worship rock in place of moon.
Their seasons last a century;
A drop of rain is a lagoon.
Their feast days come each millenium;
They say we rush to celebrate too soon.

What they honor happens slowly,
As coal that, made from color's lack,
With pressure, forms a crystal,
Creating rainbows from the color black.
This kind of change is what they worship,
Is why I took so long in coming back.

What is there waiting for me, after all,
In this place of myriad tongue,
Where even babies rush to change,
Where horror hurries your very young?
You say you missed me, but with this lie
You heads are hung.

When speaking truthfully, you must admit
That what is honest is your forget.
You know no words to call my flowers,
You sing no songs, and worse yet,
You make up names by which to call me,
You offer lies to pay your debt.

I know my father in the moon has told you
That I am dead, or just a wish
Of primitive people, tribes and women,
Those who have the brains of fish.
Oh, my children, but remember,
It is you who serve these brains on silver dish.

No, do not fear me or my anger;
Your own justice, I can see,
Is now already reaped upon you,
Upon your land, and sky, and sea.
You are dying quickly, and you speed so well.
I have returned; now you descend, replacing me in hell.

Artemis

At nine I climb
out of bed,
blue morning air
in my arms,
the harness wrapped
around hips,
the chalk attached,
and I walk,
setting moon on my right,
toward the mountain.

I begin to climb,
each step a grief
I leave behind.
Cypress roots
become my anchors
as I wade deeper
into the height
of mourning.
I am an orphan,
escaped from the arms
of my childhood,
unable to leap
to the next
expected step
of womanhood.

So I cling,
hand to rock,
foot to rock,
hand to rock,
foot to rock,
to the rhythm
of my solitude.
There are no thoughts,
only the finite
challenge of gravity
that I, inch
by inch, outwit.

Shekhina

like a moth in daylight
I see you everywhere
and rotate on the axis
of your absence

I search your name
in indices and omens
jealous when I meet
others who know you

she is mine, I want
to say, and call up the night
in the underground room
you smiled at me

I remember your face
shrouded in long dark hair
as you stood through the gates
of the camp I was leaving

you let me go
and now I know
you had to stay
for the dying

could it be that you let
me go into life, that this
silence I hear is the
sound of my choice

could it be that you believe
in me, even when I hear
nothing, even when I
wonder if you're dead

could it be that you are
my beloved, who will come
to me only in my dreams
where I can't touch you

I am a moth, mother,
smother me in something
other than air, let me land
on your white moon flower

The dust rises from the land

for the people of Chiapas

The dust rises from the land like a woman
de la cama, a slender line of light brown air
that swirls in anger at the morning sun.
There are no answers to the questions
that a thousand pieces of the earth
might ask, and do, yet still the open
hand of wonder shows the sky
its palm. Like a woman, tierra y cielo
cry out for water, and when it rains
then rest will come. Until the season
of this settling, not even night lies down
to sleep. The trees, like soldiers, hover over
as, one by one, another woman gets up to greet
la luna llena where all her secrets keep.

To Soldiers

When you bleed like we do, perhaps
you will let your weapons rest,
learn to heal like we do. Until then,

we bind you up in cycles,
when you dance with death
at the dark of every moon.

And this is what you must remember:
we never tire. We never tire of touching,
of loving, of alleviating pain.

All the wars and all the wounds
have only given women work to do.
No despair and never weary,

we bind you up in cycles
and dance our life dance
at the dark of every moon.

Wild

Actions planned are never completed.
Democritus

No one plans the roll of a wheel,
spokes clicking down the hill
in summer. Or the first violet
bloom in the spring. No one
puts this on a calendar, saying,
here is when it must be done.
The first lead crunching underfoot,
the smell of frost, the shooting star.
The dream, the kiss, the laugh,
the death, the change that bursts
and brings another season.

What the mother means to say

So here you are, early afternoon
in your life. Not evening.
Not midday. You still have a long way.
You only just came from morning.
Not to rush you, just to say:
Take it easy. Don't worry.
The sun has vowed to stay.
A yellow butterfly will keep you
company, with the chirping
cardinal outside your door.
The wind will blow
through your window.
You need nothing more.
So sit down. Get to work.
Do what you are here to do.
Not for glory, riches,
fame or fortune. Only
for the gift of being you.

Each Day

I know now why God
has counted every hair
on our heads. To love
this much is the work
of a parent. I count
each strand of auburn
and the delicate white
underneath and the
chestnut on the back
of your neck.
I stop at 2000,
the day is almost
gone. I must begin
again tomorrow.
And then night
comes, the hush
of black, and we
sleep, belly to belly,
together and breathe
into each other,
preparing, exhausted,
to begin all over again.

Dos Marias

It was in a quiet white
underground room
of the Museo Nacional
on my last day
in Ecuador that I saw her:
the pregnant virgin,
Maria Embarazada,
her chin slightly chipped,
but belly softly rounded
off in wood, made smooth
by many bruises.
The only other was in Spain,
a sign said.

I could get to her
if I followed a red
string straight across the middle
of the world to another
who waits, and wonders
what happened to her sisters,
all the other Marys who did not survive,
who, embarazadas,
were then destruidas. Destruidas,
a sign read.

Only dos Marias remain,
separated by two worlds
like the double meanings
of all the words in the same
body: embarazada, pleine,
schuld, float, sink, long,
the list goes on and on.

Gaia

I see the world stretched out
in concrete highways of abandon
over rivers, through forests,
unaware of the land they're on.

This is my life: these roads
filled with exit ramps.
I can escape repeatedly
but never once advance.

An unexpected call came through
yesterday, and then I had some hope.
I thought perhaps it was an offer
of a job for me, a place to cope.

But it was another part-time gig
without benefits or desk.
Seems no one wants the talents
of a goddess when temps can do the rest.

But I digress. I was saying
that my body is a mess.
A job won't help, I know.
And it may do less.

Imagine, if you will,
the billboard: GAIA, STRAIGHT AHEAD
CLEAN RESTROOMS, GOOD FOOD,
$1.09 FOR UNLEADED.

You laugh, but it would be nice
to have a rest stop for my bones.
A place where people could admire my beauty
while they use the telephones.

Silly daydream, ancient lady,
while standing with the whores,
as we wait for dinner to be signaled
through the open Salvation Army doors.

Green is the color where winter dreams

Green is the color where winter dreams
that white will die forever like the silence of a moth
who rests upon the wooden windowsill below the frost.
I dream that I am grown, that all these sadnesses will melt
in the summer of becoming woman, mother, keeper
of my own house, where moths do not die inside
from too much heat, where windows are always open
and the wind drifts in with smells of trees.
Outside the window the grass is never buried
under from its shame, and the leaves are never dressed
in brilliant colors for their death, where I never have to hold
my breath at the calling of my name before the entrance
of the house, where coats are never necessary
and they never hang in closets filled with poison
and I never am eight years old again, looking
out the window with a moth who lies dying,
imagining the other side of pain,
and if the next season ever really comes in green.

Walking the Boundary
for Cathy

We walk the outer edges of the land
where I live, where you visit,
what I give. Not sisters, lovers,
even friends, we measure time
by what you've taught me,
what I've left behind. You turn,
an ear to the sky, and say,
That sound, is it a dove?
No, I say, knowing the cry
of mourning well. I guide you
to the northern side, reach up
and pull down purple blossoms.
These are wisteria. Smell them.
I show you now, and we go
inside to find a crystal vase
for all we have collected.

Lakshmi

Water petals on a lotus hold within them all I need:
the clear sky of leaving, the pink inside of dreams.
I call to you while you are sleeping. Wake, I say,
and go. Clean the floors of your new palace.
Become what you will know. Dig beneath the fig tree,
tearing out each weed. Pursue black dirt
until you are bleeding, your fingers red and dripping
new life onto little seeds. It is the price I ask
of your desire, the deal I make with greed:
You will work until your skin sheds twice,
until you are not who you thought you'd be.
And in this incarnation, I will give you
what your former self did want. Instead
of pleading for another, you will fall
upon your knees, now freed. Holy Lady,
you will cry, Great Sage, All Praise.
For you will know, from work and age,
blood and shedding, that what we gain here
comes from other lifetimes, and often oddly fits.
Still you know that blessing is required.
Still you know that this is all there is.

Return

She is shining
white light
white stars
white moon.
Her glory
glows over
us all
as we sleep.
Her power
so strong
it touches
even men.
See, in the morning,
how this one
brings food
for the family.
That one,
see him
kiss his son.
See another
cry when night
descends.
She is coming,
every evening,
and everyone
knows it.
Even the men.
So great
is her love
for us all.

Yemaya

I hold in my hands your water, cupped
over the breaking waves. It releases
from my finger with the wind.

I hold my palms against the wind
and feel your tiny sand drops sway
from my skin and back again.

I let my body enter your waves, warm
with the sun, and bubble, bounce,
and then sink back into your arms.

A baby, belly down and head up,
I crawl over you and you let me
rock upon your breasts, then you tire.

You make me stand to receive your hand
against my face to remind me
that I am only part of you.

I lie back, let my face go under
slightly, feel you hold me up and
rock me, lift me, drop me, love me.

Your salt is salve for my healing
and I let it sting my wounds,
and begin to suck my terror.

Loving takes a rhythm, you teach me
on the shore of your body, giving
wholly, then going out again.

Waiting for the next round, I look up
and see your shy lips, in the dark
around the moon, kiss in bloom.

Your breast, the water, your face,
the night, I leave you for the land
so I can sleep, and wake, and plan.

Freya

You ask me if I remember when we last talked,
how you were married, I was not.

Now I am married, and you are not.

We measure our years like tree trunks,
by our marriages.

I tell you this and you laugh.
You say you have to leave and you run
into the cold rain on a northern Friday night,
slipping into the seat of a cat-driven cab.

Here in this tribe of translucent women
difference is not the problem.
We, like wolves,
caught in steel traps,
love those outside the cage
and chew on our own bodies
to be freed
from our own caught parts.

Often it takes some time
to see what is broken and missing
under skirts
when we meet members of our tribe
on foreign streets.

We walk away from each other
and pretend to strangers
that our stumbles are erotic
steps in dance halls back home.

We make people laugh
when we talk
backwards
about home.

We never go home
our fear is too great
of finding pieces of ourselves,
parts of legs and ears and tails,
strewn across the roads
as we drive back into town.

The only limbs on our body's tree
we cannot chew are our teeth
so we hide them under slender lips
and ferociously refuse to smile
or to eat.

Oh, my mean,
unsmiling sister,
you are so thin
and you walk
so crookedly.

Wouldn't you like,
just once,
like a cypress in the wind,
to lean
against me.

I could hold you.
I would share my heat
so generously.

Late January

Branches fall back
away, midwinter,
to make room
for the sky. The grey
underbelly
coming down on us,
asleep. Held by leaves,
by the weather
of drought and questions
of cats, waiting
for spring, waiting
for more: the certainty
of seasons, the rest
of change, the hope
of endings, the scorn
of the same.

Branches fall away
from fingertips
and eyelashes,
from pinetrees
and plans,
from finality
and loathing,
leaving us
to stand.
Shy and bare
against the belly
of the sky,
we settle in
for warming.
Pale and fair
against the shedding

and the sigh,
we surrender
patiently
to growing.

Desire

What we want to satisfy is what comes
easily out of the blue, the desire of wet
dew on green grass at dawn that yearns
for a finger of eastern sun to touch down
upon it, a craving carved into glass
upon a night window, the letters
in a language unknown to the neighbors,
counting time by calendars from another
land, waiting for the film to be over
so that our real lives can begin again.

Facing

Deep within me is a still place without geography.
It expands endlessly and yet goes no where.
It is the opposite of motion. I thought it was an ocean
that could take me under, and I couldn't swim.
It came to me first when I was afraid, and I
was a child, so I associated it with fear.
It took me all these years to discover it was fear's
opposite. It took me that long to learn to face it.

2006

2016

Light My Way

Fire of illumination, light my way this day.

May I walk in beauty, may beauty surround
what I do and what I say.

What is closest is not most important.
Even bees know when a further flower needs a fill.

Help me see my powers of transformation,
regeneration, hope, and will.

Give me comfort in my questions,
and guide my faith.

Give me vision in the nighttime
as I run through trees of faith.

Morning Glories in Alabama

The best things in my garden were not planted by me.
Yesterday I walked along the edge of Alabama and saw
morning glories on the red road. Some were light,
with pink centers, others purple, bursting forth.
I'd planted them for years near my front porch, but
they never came back like that.

And then I went home to Carolina. A yellow blooming
beanstalk had grown up in my absence, and crawling up
its spine were green hearts and periwinkle faces. What
I'd wished for had come true.

I received morning glory blessings, in the heart of my
own yard, just by being who I am, not because of what
I did or didn't do.

What the Tree Has Seen

In the middle of a city park
women gather with each other
near an ancient magic tree
and sing of what the tree has seen.

In the south, a woman sings of eyes
stabbed open, and of other eyes sewn shut,
while beneath the morning sky of blue,
children played on swings and pigeons cooed.

No one moved when in the north a woman
screamed, her teeth and tongue torn wide,
her grey tone rising til it turned to stone
and, wailing, fell upon the ground nearby.

In the west, a woman kept a constant rhythm,
laying bare hands against the wood,
with heavy patience, as only a mother,
mourning her weaning child, could.

Still in the east there stands an ancient woman,
who calls upon the spirit with upraised hands
of five-fingered yellow leaves in autumn light.

She prays to bring back breath to all those
still sleeping, or dead, or not quite,
as day descends and turns the tree to night.

Moonlit, the women stand in silence
and raise a toast to all the tree has seen.
They are drunk in honor of her memory,
what makes possible the songs they sing.

Bunk Bed in the Holocaust Museum

A way on wood, the heart, beat, down,
lies scribbled, carved, broken
what the tides, swift, drown,
where women squeezed, freezing,
in November snow.

Poems still survive
long after women poets die,
after scraping bloody
fingernails across German oak
and elder, pine.

Caskets and casks of wine
are made of wood, what time
ripens, saves for history,
fastens fire, holy,
rides the grace of endless sea.

A half century's bed now
lies encased in a museum,
under guard, entrance granted
with her permission,
after all that still cannot be said:

Poetry, which dimly fades on wood,
smells of heat and violence,
tears the mask from silence,
lone survivor,
canoe that floats eternally.

In the Hospital at White Sands

Once I walked the halls of White Sands,
winced at yellow light, smelled the fire in her room,
flesh destroyed by winds as hot as heaven,
smashed together, fried apart.
They left a crater people visit, at her heart.

But bruises being bitter and contained,
still her body beats. Her legs, pale and bare,
move below the heavy sheets in summer,
slow as sand. When I say that I am ready,
she waves with one cold hand.

There are trees on her ceiling.
They survived, come back green
and bear cherries every year.
On her breast burst wildflowers,
thick from every crevice,
a violet, pink, and yellow necklace
that gives her vivid dreams,
waking her with endings,
sweet like we have never seen.

Calling It Down

Call down an ending to all this:
the motors whirring, engines
running, alarms beeping,
trucks squealing, chains sawing,
fires igniting, claws digging,
everywhere earth ripping.

Bring every bare hand to the
ground again and again
until there is an enormous
hole to pile all the machines
in. Let them crunch and
ground and sing a death song
as they go in. Cover them
with silent earth. Say no
prayers. Say no thing. Hold
your breath if you can.
Listen. Hear the silence
filling up the world again.

What Happens Outside When Poets Read

Daffodils outside the window open dry mouths to the rain.
We know each other in this room. Out there we make it up.

Two birds land in a tree, the branches almost naked
in the waning day. The devil on my left shoulder is only

a shadow from my head. The two birds keep returning as
poets keep reading. Their words are wings that take us back

to things that hold us through seasons, dry and wet, naked
and budding, bursting and letting go. Each breath is a death

we allow. Our words are telling how we have been dying with
devils and shadows on the way to this day. We are a moment

on a calendar, but birds there are their own timeless weather,
beyond symbol or sin, setting of suns or the saving of oceans.

There are no words for what might save this earth. Still we
keep breathing. Still we keep seeing a reason to keep speaking

word after word, death after death. Happiness sleeps in the
in-between of sunset and stop. We do not know if we will

make it through, and if we do, what we will be. Our skin is
fragile and yellow. We touch each other with a gentle pop of

yes, world, sleep, awake, love, again, day, bird, tree, when, we.

The Rock Speaks

I am a rock, the soil drowns my skin, I have known
the rise and fall of civilizations like ocean tides. Come. Go.
My hair is lichen, hunger a solid mass pulling gravity to me,
the longing for an end to worry. I am a table where poverty
is served for lunch. Underneath me is a child. She hides. She
cries. I tell her to stand up. Victory is not the same as win-
ning, I say. Not the same as wealth. Not the same as fame.
Every storm has its beginning. Abundance moves in clouds.
Learn to praise the soil. Learn to praise the rain.

On the question of Jonah, whales, and the weight of a woman

I've never connected with Jonah.
That big whale story. Swallowing.
Fear of the sea. All that.

I guess it's because I've been fat.
I am the Jonah. I scare men
with my abdomen. Belly.

I love to eat. I love meat.
Chewing. Caramel. Craving.
The salt. The fat. The sugar.

Popcorn has been my Communion.
I take it nightly, like Holy Bread.
But not with wine. I like beer.

I don't have much fear.
Of food. Of being big. Of the ocean.
I swim in these things.

They are me. They are good. I wonder if God
fears Jonah. Or women. Or bellies.
I doubt it. Maybe he should.

Sonnet for My Daughter at 9

Scared of sonnets, though I never did one,
Skipped most hard parts: science, math—
So when her homework turns hard, I hum
My old song of triumph—and its aftermath—

I did not sing my childhood as a tragedy—
Had no words then, so I'd never dare
Failing. And now I face my past postfactly—
Admitting there was never anyone there.

By nine I'd been raped at least once, as I've said,
In letters that float across my brain and bounce—
Watched him on top of her as she said no in red—
I still see all of this, despite years in and out

Of therapy. See, if after this I can do a sonnet,
You can, too: Hear the hard part and then sing above it.

The Skin of Your Hand

The skin of your hand is paper
where dark words were written
by us, mother and daughter, together.
What we had, your dad and I, is over.
I look out the window at coming
green grass, and my anger
is gone. I am full with what
his eyes gave me when he gave me
you. I cannot pretend any more.
My mouth of soft mothering words
is empty now, and you are dark
in the silence. Spring comes fast,
my daughter. But for now, it is winter
and we are no longer together.
The snow is white like a ceiling.
Take the skin of your hand and
write the words upon it. Continue
what I began. Begin with the feelings.

Let Go

Your hands are bleeding from holding on so needy to what
is broken and busted open. These shards can't hold wine or
even old letters or time. Time to let go. Part the sand with
your fingers and feel it release its grip of covering, despite
your fear hovering and threatening with the thunder of past
regret. This is for you to get. Broken glass becomes jewels
after thousands of years and you don't have that long. Put
it down. Don't kneel. Walk away. Sing your song. Feel the
cuts on your perfectly shaped, painful fingers begin to heal.

Spring Equinox, Sunday Morning

Facing east, waiting for sunrise between the cedars and palmetto tree. A pink glow. Caw from a crow. Mockingbird stands perch with her low grinding purr on the cedar while another rustles in the palmetto – babies already maybe. Woodpecker in the west, knocking the morning awake. Jet trail blends with the clouds on the horizon, a milky blanket over the strawberry sky. Mockingbirds trade places, then both go in, one gathers palmetto berries, the other looks in on the nest. Tangerine enters the sky. All the buds are about to pop – apple, white, and cherry, pink. I am thinking about the future – a vision of revision – how long it took me to be patient – as if the lesson could only be learned by practicing it myself. Gold glows. The sunrise takes a long time to happen. It does not come all at once. We think it does, asleep, in our beds. When we are awake, we see the long history everything takes to come into this moment. Woodpecker winds up. Blue and white touch down from the sky. The clouds mottle like a cold baby's skin. The light gathers from within. The scar of the jet is faded, smaller yet, as time heals even the largest regret. Geese flock in the distance. This used to be a swamp, and at dawn, you can smell the damp and a hint of the salt from a prehistoric shore. We do not always really know what we want. Sometimes when we give up wanting, home gives us more.

Blossom

You tell me you are
not sure what you
are doing, sitting
in the cave of your
old life. I take your
hand and say, come
on, let's open
to the light
just dawning
like a knife.

Spring is late
and reluctant
this year, but
we light our
breath--
breathe
in, breathe out,
in cold spring air,
and know that
she is near.

Two weeks later,
the blossoms on
the cherry tree
have bloomed
and everything
around me has
exploded, and
I hear the echo
of the boom and
I don't run.

I am here, says
spring, as bees
buzz in the pink,
and all new life
begins with an
implosion-- this began
long ago within--
like my sap that
flowed last year and
had to slow.

This is your
time of blossom.
Beyond in or ex
plosion-- beyond yes
or no-- into everything
you came here for
and are now
doing. So, flower, do
what you know. Do it.
Flow.

Begun in Love

May night dark breeze
        flies through the screen
                candle glows
                        tea cold
                                blanket from Germany
                                        wrapped
                                                around my thighs.

And I am not this.
                                Or that.

Just as this is not exactly night
                        but the final rest
                                before the morning
                                        dawns
                                        a day

that will end with my daughter and
                        mother and
                                woman lover
                                with me

on the land where the trees and creek
                have sheltered me.
                        I have called this home.

It is not this.
                                Or that.

It is the green turning earth
                that swells
                        with the tides

of our birth
and
connects
to the blood in me,
the sea
of what I am worth.

This round world.
This body.
This mother-daughter
journey.

Begun in love, resting through
the night in love like grasses
that cry dew drops
until the morning
and let birds drink
from their tears.

All love is wet and small and giving
like this.

It is this.

And that.

Juice

The Buddhists say let go know
you are not this pulse crave
beat need but I'm American
and born to run drum dance
have more and I want you
so bad I can taste you
swallow slow more
I used to be unlike this
my body was a cup of hot
chocolate and I would fill
her sweet and soft then
have enough fill up push
away go play outside run
away but once I had your
juice I gave up chocolate
and the tart went straight
to my heart orange lemon
pomegranate lime apricot
tangerine mine all mine
it was me I was tasting fruit
squeezed from the tree of you.

Fruit

I pull peaches
from the trees
and you say,
Put them in jars.
And I say,
What for?
The trees will
grow more.
You will, too.
Eat all you want.
There is no lack
to what you
can have.
Watch the trees
and learn
this fact:
fruit comes
every summer
wet and sweet
plump and more
than enough.
Get fat on fruit
again and again.

Spin

I hear Joan and my mother
is young again on the floor
in a spin from drinking
laughing and her boyfriend
is there with her trying to
still the floor for her and this
was my first vision of love
I wanted a man who could
do this for me I wanted to be
so drunk laughing spinning
free after leaving a man
who did such damage to me
and I tried with men but
one after one they gave
up because some women
spin so hard no floor can
ever be stilled under them
and I tried stilling myself
with pills peace therapy
but that stilled too much
in me so I left and found
a woman and she did not
try to still the floor but said
earth take her into you and
do what I cannot do and at
first I was lonely love was
something you did together
I thought but the earth taught
me that moon and sun are
far away and spin in their
own seasons and cycles and
from a distance they are
blessed and this makes
her love them no less.

Dreamwaves

The ocean is a belly
where sleep enters
again and again,
a clean blanket
after losing the
slipper and no
prince comes for
happily ever after
and no lawyer,
either, at the end.
You pick the clover
from the grass
and hold it in
your hands as
you marry yourself,
a ring of daisies
around your finger
and watch the spell
of storm come down
to quench what
you finally admit,
after years of stuck,
that you desire.
The ocean goes in
and out again.
You sleep like a baby
with dreams on fire.

The Sign

I used to wander the yard
in wonder of where, year
after year, I was going,
looking and listening
for signs and songs to
tell the way. Today I
sit still in my house,
knowing the road is
my own blood and
I am walking it daily,
the only sign I need
my own hand moving,
the only song I sing
my own breath moving.

In Between

I greet the morning light
with breath like fog, out
with the old, the night,
the dark, and hold
it there, the in-between,
the pause, where God
resides, before taking in
the day, what remains
to be seen. I may not
live there, but I try
to seek what is still
in the middle of living,
knowing peace only
comes like the clouds,
endless out, endless in.
In the midst of moving
we glimpse the bright
invisible within.

It Could Turn

It could turn to more violence, uprising
Of the voiceless, cocksure guns to replace
The throats that are choked with bullets.

It could turn to reasons, talking heads and
Shrunken necks on color TV saying, Look
At me, how smart I am, a brain, well-trained.

It could turn to prayer, together in worship
And song, gathered to mourn what is wrong
And what God might one day make right.

It could turn to symbol, stars and stripes
Half mast, confederacy at full blast, flowers,
Arm bands, badges and bumper stickers.

It could turn to theology, theories of evil
And what one should believe, pontiffs and
Preachers filling the bleachers with Amen.

It could turn to the rising of women,
Mothers who raise sons to put down guns
And pick up babies, train to be daddies.

It could turn to revolution, a turning tide
That swims with the pride of one ocean
Under water, outlaws and shark bait for all.

It could turn to memory, the heavy hand on
The heart of what could not be spoken
For generations and is now shouting out.

It could turn to tears, mourning all we can
Never be, look at the history that's not in
The books, what our heavy bodies still carry.

It could turn to silence, something melted
After fire, wet truth and the wire of walking
Over coals that still smolder with justice.

And it could turn to each of us, saying What
Now, you Americans who love to choose,
What will you do? It could be up to you.

The Train at Night

The train at night shakes our house.
Windows rattling like champagne flutes
and I feel your body turn in the dark
away from Germany and the dreams
of old trains. I place my hand on your
hip, and it's warm like an oven.
One day the trains will stop coming.
First, robins will search for worms.
Then vines will twine through rails.
Even the stories of trains will be silent.
And our house, quiet like after a party,
will wait for our bodies to make the
glasses sing from the cabinets again.

How White Women Live in South Carolina

Sunlight rusted through the hinges of existence
in the early spring after seasons of rain
on the morning we came from dreams of drowning.
You and I are still alive in the state where nine
were shot down four days after our wedding.
As women, we love in the aftermath of massacre.
Rust red brick dirt showed through white washed walls
in the early morning after months of silence
on the spring day we woke to hear poetry.
You and I are not yet deaf in the room where words
rise and split their heads against the concrete and we claim
the blood coming down like holy wine with our tongues.

This is Not a Resurrection

This is not a resurrection
We wanted it to be
We pulled back the cave stone
Of who we were
What they did
We called them on it
We went to search
For who we now could be

This is not a resurrection
It was the women who did this
Women who wept
Washed feet
And covered the face
And dark bodies
That carried the cross
Like water and wood
Without enough break or wine
Holding most of the weight
Time after time

This was not a resurrection
There was no gathering
And showing of the palms
No one could agree
Upon the meaning
Of safety
Or how to pin
Proper blame
So while we waited
For tongues
To stop wagging
And holy breath
To arrive

We admit
This is not a resurrection
And we return to rake
The leaves
Left lying
Since last week
And their colored bodies
Begin to pile
Like flowers
At a funeral
That smell too sweet
And do their time
Standing in for those
Who are still living
But could not be present
As a family
In this fire
And the sympathy
Bouquets wait patiently
For their turn
In the pyre
To rise

Wedding Women

The green gallbladder twitches and the dog
Gnaws an antler as the bed sheets grow
Wet with saliva and our brains work in rooms
Next to each other while the thunder rolls in
Without rain and we must make our own.

We must make our own we know it now
Even though it took us years to learn it
We had to taste it with our own tongues
From the silence and the yessing to the
Hims who said they loved us like lords.

They loved us like lords and we were
Maidens vessels cups carpets spoons
That fed them food not money and bodies
Became the bridge where they crossed
Into us and burnt down our villages.

Burnt down our villages until the ashes
Filled our mouths and we called it candy
And paid for it with our labor silence eyes
Closed against our own desires even the
Words our and own and desires were gone.

Desires were gone and we walked away
While the maps caught fire and our shoes
Melted in the fine sunlight of one new day
That held hope and light fed us with atoms
We had never tasted anything so sweet.

Anything so sweet must be digested and
We took our time and chewed sometimes
For each other because we would get tired
And need to dream this new world of bodies
Without bridges and fires we lit ourselves.

We lit ourselves with moonlight like teeth
That shine in smile beds without locks where
Everything is free and we have more
Than enough money because it was a lie
There wasn't enough that was the chain.

That was the chain we tied across our wrists
And then tried to flap our wings and when
We realized this flight became possible as
This green gallbladder twitches like a girl
In a womb giving birth to herself gently.

Herself gently opening the hand to another
Who holds a ring and they take turns while
The equal of it is a vow that heals their
Tongues bodies mouths fires teeth beds
Money wrists wings wombs girls women.

2017

Water

It started slow and mellow
an acoustic chord of lullaby
and the century gone by
but then drum beat began
like your heart and the night
when fear woke like a flood
and you felt your blood
rising and threatening
yet somehow you got up
and used your legs and
pulled milk from the shelf
ignoring the sloshing
like a rocking ship
because you couldn't
quite locate the source
in all this water and
you checked the weather
and almost wished for a
hurricane or signal
of warning of what is
coming because there
are no straight roads
anymore and everything moves
in boats now and you never
did learn how to navigate
so you stare at the stars
and long for ancient
memory that ancestors
once did carry but that
too is drowned and you
are amazed to be still
floating with the logs
and nests and cars that

wash by and we are all
going in the same direction
but we can't see the end
whether waterfall or ocean
so you hold to the sound
of your heart like a locket
in the grand crescendo
and know this chord will
stay in the memory of
those who dive deep
enough to find it in the
sand at water's end
surrounded by the last
bed of coral and a few
fish made so colorful
by their survival that
you cannot even now
imagine how they shine
at the bottom of the sea
with their bodies of rainbow.

Walls

This is a poem about walls
and how water can breach
and the destruction of this
and what it can teach

We can bang our heads
we can pray and preach
we can wish them away
but nothing will reach

The power of walls
comes from inside
how they hold within
a place we can hide

Walls are like tongues
that land in the trees
a magical singing
the lyrics of need.

Flood

Countertops riddled with plastic forks and paper plates
open water bottles closed crates waiting to be consumed

Over muddy floors and torn out walls and neighbors
giving sympathy saying There but for the grace

Lower sandbags to the ground hear the sound of sirens
coming closer wonder when this will be over

No one knows even while the cameras are rolling
hoping no one sees your heart already broken

Last looks at sodden photo books the grief a sandwich
left stale in the sun chew and swallow till it's done

After this is digested as a memory there will be a day
when it feels far away and you will have a story

Go to bed and when you wake you will taste forgetting
on your tongue knowing you have a body and it has a heart

Some people use faith and others need bourbon but you go
to the kitchen amidst clutter and make coffee like a rampart

Coffee

I sit at the table
so tired wanting
to go back to bed.

She brings me coffee
and bread. Eat,
she says. Tired

Is another kind
of hungry.
It happens

When our hands
are empty,
we have nothing

To give. Now
is the time
for accepting.

Take this food.
Take this drink.
Take my body.

Take me as your
wife, caretaker,
beloved.

Be animal.
Be fed.
Make your life

Here, with me.
Sleep by my
human feet.

America

We are watching Angels in America
and I ask you if you would hate
me if I left you if you were dying
and you say yes and I say I wouldn't
I don't mean I wouldn't leave
I mean that I wouldn't hate
you I would want you to escape
the pain the shit the mess
the vomit the night sweats
the tender the smell the ache
the tears the pills the powders
the doctors the lawyers the
insurance forms the formula
the spoons the swallows the
anger the end the sorrow and
you say I'm lying but I'm
not because this is America
and you came here from
Germany and we both know
what it means not to be free.

Kiss

If this were the last kiss, I wouldn't
cling, I wouldn't cry, I wouldn't try
to recreate that bliss of first with
the wind off the lake and wet of
water and touch that lingered
past the sun and helped it rise
again when night was done.

If this were the last kiss, I would
be soft, I would smile, I would let
go to create the grief of ending
when the wind slows for good
after a storm and all the land
becomes water in the flood.

If this were the last kiss, I would
already be writing the memory
in my mind even as I am saying
goodbye because it is the fierce
power of the imagination which,
as it says in the Kabbalah, was
the gift that led us to each other.

If this were the last kiss, I would
open my mouth and let the soft
wet tongue come out to tease you,
not like a lover because that will
be over, but like a childhood
friend saying, Nanny, Nanny,
booboo, you can't catch me,
and you will be it and I'll hide
here in the bushes in this old
body until you tag me.

Sunday

The Sunday train is long and
fast and empty heading for
the coast to fill with cargo
from China and most foreign
countries where we cannot
imagine lives as stories but
only Leonard Cohen songs
that croon so lonely deep and
running like a black man in
the street before dawn trying to
get his healthy on before the
sun comes up with traffic smoke
and busy on the way to church to
pray for forgiveness on behalf of
every single one of us in this country.

Winter

Sometimes people say to sad that it's easy to be happy
this is like telling winter to be summer and during the
black branch of frozen the bud is an imagination
cold fingers lie across the bark like barbed wire
clouds come down like prison guards to make sure
sun doesn't touch anyone in a cell and it's easy to say
we are free and the theology of will has a history
of centuries and heavy volumes of redemption but
from the weather of winter the whole world is frozen.

Priest

I wanted to be a priest but I didn't
want to give up Catholic so I just quit
church

and created circles under moon
and stars and swirling sun and women
singing

despite my desire I'd eaten a whole tree
of apples but Eden wouldn't give me
talent

so I married a priest who didn't like apples
but she could sing and knew Greek and I
knelt.

Reverberating

Five minutes before her alarm
goes off I plug in the electric
guitar and press my fingers
against the strings and sing
like she does neck back open
releasing vultures and
screaming stay away stop
eating on my flesh it's bad
enough what happened and

It's over now because songs
do end that's why we love
them and the rhythm tells
us heartbeats can sustain
ticking clocks and righteous
loss and silence after dreaming

And sound is the evidence
that we survived and our
tongues still taste the bitter
but the waves they crash
into the night and somewhere
still are always reverberating.

Artist

There is a woman in the second century
who waits in a stone tomb for some relief
and there is a baby behind her watching
with his little penis peeking out by her thigh
and he pets an animal while waiting to be fed
and she has a plate of food but it is by her belly
and an angel is reaching up to grab a piece of fruit
and maybe there is another baby inside her from the
oval of pleats that surrounds her in the half shell and the
words below the sculpture say that this is a painter in her
studio but there are no brushes or canvas or space or peace

Pray

When you repeat those words in the middle of the night
it is not your tongue speaking in trees but all the women
who have ever prayed like this with children sleeping
and animals nearby staying quiet while her heart hangs
like a wet sweater on the wooden shelf dripping syllables
sounds over and over until sense becomes nonsense
and everything breaks down breaks like the stove heater
washer river marriage body womb baby friend foundation
ground roof shingles windows walls door branch beds
glass pans bowls spoons cups blender coffee pot lunch
plans fruit bruised fish gone bad milk rancid toes on
fire hip flaring up and the knee heart lung nose head
bones muscles back fingers eyes throat breath whole
house whole body all the beings all the land and animals
all the food preparation all the chewing and swallowing
all digestion elimination wiping washing carrying away
downstream flowing transformation dredging clearing
creating flow back again all this woman prays for
words tumbling like spitting vomiting yelling screaming
for help but no sounds come out and eventually she
is filled with a silence that stuffs her like a down
comforter or marble chiseled from the mountain of
her body and placed over her to say stay stay stay
you will not fall you will not fall apart you will not
fall away you will not fall over you can do this another day.

Leave

On the last night of the darkest moon we circle in an underground room and speak the words of all the times we've left before saying goodbye or sneaking out screaming or silent or talking it out or just slipping under instead of taking a knife to the throat and we listen and do not judge because we have all left like this in cars we owned or borrowed trains buses the diesel drug in the middle of the night to keep us awake as we waited sitting on luggage and no matter the age we will all leave this star eventually because when we circle like this and have the courage to see from a long perspective we admit that we are made of stars and all stars are made from distance.

Tamales

I want to make tamales with you
I don't know how to do it
I will have to be taught
Someone must show me how to use
My hands
The corn is like paper
A skin you can write on
And the beans have ink
The meat drips juice
This is how we use our voices

I want to make tamales with you
I've never done it
I'm sure that it goes slow
Like this pen on this page
And we must resist
The microwave
Because too much fast has hurt us
Burned tongues
Scorched fingers
Until we could not feel
To mourn or rage

I want to make tamales with you
You would think eating would be
The best part
But it's not
It's waiting for the oven to get hot
And talking so quietly
Beyond thought
And bumping into each other
Leaning into the kitchen
In the same spot
And when that song comes on
Dancing

Earth

Earth wakes early and moon
is still partying – her kids are
with the ex for the weekend
and earth waves, doesn't
want to stop moon dancing
and moon, polite, turns
the music down a bit.

Earth makes coffee and a to-do
list etched on the blossoming
pear tree where the water
rises joyfully and the wood
is moist and soft for writing:
save seeds migrate geese
build nests clean rivers
cool oceans grow grass
filter carbon bake a cake
before the rain make beavers
sign the contract for the dams
call hummingbirds
to check their ETA
pay rent in full to the sun
before the fifth– remember
you were late last month
and there was no winter.

Earth bakes biscuits after
finishing her list and moon
is heading home to bed
but earth knows she never
really sleeps just tosses
and turns and tries to close
her eyes and earth doesn't
know which is worse—
to be a woman doing all
the work to keep things
going or the best friend
with not much power
of her own who has to sit
back as she unravels and
everything unfolds in this
uphill battle and watch.

Resist

Resist the demon demanding pay in the form
of guilt or performance near the fires that threaten
melt your fair sense with wax to harden into up
good down bad go leave wait stay get going join
the parade walk if you must take the road by the river
the Romans left so you won't lose your way
shake the bells as you let yourself get loud
notify the authorities you are coming
refuse to lift the stone hold the door do the bidding
hurt strain obey listen bow down any more.

Dive

I once thought revolution was like drowning
and I stood at the edge of an oil tanker and
contemplated jumping down where the whales
would carry my body below into a secret grotto
where effigies of humans floated in effervescent
light but I couldn't go so I wouldn't be able
to see any of this and even if I did go only
my soul would know they loved me and
the spirit part of me would hear the songs
the whales would sing for me and I didn't
have a plan for what happened next because
death teaches to let go and whales float
because they've learned so and that's when
I realized I didn't have to die or dive to
have a revolution and I turned around on
that tanker and walked right up to the captain
saying give me the keys to the engine room
I am driving from now on and as he dropped
them into my palm I could hear whale song.

Courage

People of good courage,
a cat named Nicki Minaj
sat next to me under a Scorpio
waning moon as forces waged
outside the window between
branches of government and oak
the light that came in was
not available to the human
eye except through lines
and grids and codes of human
making of such complexity
that machines could work
on their own velocity. We
remember bodies and language
are other kinds of codes and the word
courage comes from the French
coeur, which means heart.
When we get quiet we can hear
her persistence resistance insistence
assistance existence deep in our core.

Human

Sometimes I try to imagine
being the only one alive
not that there was an ending
from war or watershed
but that I've just been born
and everyone is still waiting
in the wings of rivers and
streams to tap the spring
called human and for this
dark moment I am the only
quiet and cool there are no
news shows or histories
or arguments or even talking
because I haven't opened
my mouth yet and nothing
has surprised hurt amazed
wounded left abandoned me
I am the only one who can
do these things to myself
and what would be the reason
when there is nothing that is
missing but I can't sustain this
vision for long because my
body calls hunger thirst
pain release an endless list
of demands and I remember
that even if I were the first
person on earth I wouldn't be
alone there would be my
body and this is when I open
my mouth and begin to speak.

March

I want to write a poem but I'm angry and
gone are references to my existence and
marriage on the White House website and
Joni nailed it when she said you don't and
it's gone in a code and a puff of smoke and
there is a man behind the curtain and
he is coming for the queers and women and
immigrants and Muslims and blacks and
artists and scholars and schools and
thinkers and poor and sick and woke and
the sun is not yet up but I am and
I am pulling back that curtain and
showing the world his wanker and
he is not going to scare me and
everyone will see his dick,
so little compared to our pussies.

Today

Some days you wake up and it's
morning and the sun comes
running like he's on a race track
and the oval is all he can
handle over and over in
the same circle and you join
the wheel like a hamster
coffee commute school work
clock rush late early be
somewhere for the duty
or the money and the day
ends much the same home eat
drink numb watch laundry
bedtime alarm sleep toss turn
but not today because yesterday
on every body of land on the
planet women gathered our bodies
and marched laughed sang
listened spoke stood held
hands hugged loved each
other and ourselves like
we always wanted every
day but finally did and so
every day after is today.

Feminist

We were not shrill we didn't
shriek yell whine complain
we sang a song in the gentle
and it was about the nation
but as we filled up the city
like a womb preparing for
conception other women were
gathering all over the globe
and this diversity of snow
rain tropic desert plain
city park yard was the point
because the earth has crevices
rivers mountains waterfalls
swamps muds oceans cliffs
places high and low and one
body so we climbed her
like a tree in one body and
millions in difference was
strength and beauty and
ecology family community.

Temple

It wasn't that hard after all thousands
of years simply rolled like a stone
down to this moment when down
became up and we rose up in
the temple like the one who over
turned the tables but we were
not watching the toppling
we were not waiting for him
because he did what he could
and then left and did the most
even came back again to show
you don't need evidence to know
your own power showed palms
to the doubter because the body
is the only evidence we need
to know we are here and alive
and living and breathing and
giving and hurting and healing
and leaving and grieving and
praying and staying and
together we are the temple.

Mud

Oh Anne Sexton I wish you could see what we've done there are dogs
on our bed and bunnies in the sun and I remember how your puppies
brought you back to life and everything was a hopeful poem at the end
of a chain of pain and your publisher made you write it and truth did get
seeded with syllables because there are daughters who have courage
and don't pull on their mothers and women who love each other gentle
and space where there is a spring filled with clear water and mud
is something we roll in on our own skin when we make the decision.

Trust

Trust is a handshake with your own hands.
You let go of the rope you are holding
or hanging from and begin to put one palm
into another palm. Pay yourself first
with the soft money of your own skin.
Take out an insurance policy on the
voice within. Coin by coin, drop your
worth into the jar of your heart and
feel the equity begin. You are not a
commodity. You are kith and kin.

Quiver

Yesterday my wife played with my mother's dog
throwing the tennis ball from the kitchen to the
family room again and again making her happy
and animals have fewer words and more love
than humans until she said something is wrong
with the dog her jaw was quivering and I said
maybe she's had too much and my mom said
no she just does that and so my wife knelt down
put the ball down petted her and kept her distance
because dogs don't always like to be hugged
it takes their power away and she whispered it's
okay it's okay you can take a break you don't have
to keep going and going until you quiver.

Politics

This isn't new politics
like poetry it
takes the very old
and sits her down
at the kitchen table
with a cup of coffee
maybe it is night
and babies are sleeping
after a day that
wouldn't quit
maybe it is before dawn
and someone is gone
never to come back
maybe it is cloudy
and a small lamp
lends light to her hands
maybe it is sunny
and birds at the feeder
give them something
to look at when words
are slow in this
conversation between women
and when you refill the coffee
you don't need to be a leader
when you drink you don't
need to follow
because each body
is equal in the swallow
and we take turns serving
and being served
and this is the essence
of this politics nothing
is fixed and when
it's time we all get up
to do the dishes.

Peace

Peace slips into me like a virus
still I resist like there was a bonus
to the fight struggle plea grasping
asking someone else who I could
would should be and this is gone
no one is there the ghost of my old
self may long for support help
aid and rescue but this new self
knows there never really was
anyone here but me in the middle
of the soul fight urge for flight
brink of sanity pulled back
just before the cliff I learned
to keep one hand upon the branch
and speak of tongues in trees
until I could believe in me.

Light

Pay attention to the light moving
across the clean floor and open
baskets on the table waiting.
Sometimes you will have to
stay this way for a long time
to see it. The dog will take
a nap and then wake and stretch.
Keep watching. Something
will begin to shift and you might
catch it in your hand. It won't
stay. This is the essence of light.
And you, too, are made this way.

Here

What if there is nothing
to wait for? Not that
there is nothing, but
that it's already here.
That happiness you
hope for? Here.
That sign you look
for? Here. The peace
you search for?
Here. Here. Here.
Listen to the three
chirps of the cardinal
in the tree right
there. His song
is all you need.
Here. Here. Here.

There

What is that sound?
It is the wind in the leaves.

Why is it there?
Because it isn't yet here.

Will it come here?
Watch and listen.

I can feel it.
Sometimes that happens.

What happens?
Feeling without seeing.

Eye

In the lap of a pine tree,
I read books and hid.
The bark sang to me.
I wrote what it said.

There was a time before fear.
It lives in us still.
Hold hands. Shed tears.
Walk where you will.

Each hole is an opening.
Jump over or in.
Each eye practices focusing.
Sight lies beyond loss and win.

World

I see your boots by the bed and I shed years of straightening
up not sitting till it was right the spoon out of the sink the towel on
the rack the peanut butter capped the coat in the closet the plants
watered and animals fed but none of this straightened me so I threw
spoons until a visitor came and it was you and we threw towels
on the floor ate everything with our fingers took boxes from the
closet and let a spring come up to feed and water the world.

Bud

And then one morning there are velvet
buds on the pear tree and in the cold air
you reach your fingers to touch like the
vernix on your daughter's cheek after
birth it is white and soft and still smells
of the other world where light waves
move like toddlers dancing and music
grooves in harmony and there is no need
for faith in eternity because the heart
explodes full like a child never known
to hunger and here we call it spring or
starting over but really it is all happening
always and occasionally we get glimpses
of the circle and the shine of gold through
the ring that holds the tongues in trees.

Acknowledgments

"The Last Kiss." AuntieBellum.org 4/26/17.

"Today." voxpoetica.com 1/31/17.

"This is Not a Resurrection," "It Could Turn," and "Wedding Women." *Lady/Liberty/Lit.* December 21, 2016. https://www.ladylibertylit.com/single-post/2016/12/21/Three-Poems

"How White Women Live in South Carolina." JMWW. March 9, 2016. Reprinted in *Hand to Hand: Poets Respond to Race.* Edited by Al Black and Len Lawson. (Muddy Ford Press, 2017): 98.

"The Train at Night." One. February 24, 2016. http://one.jacarpress.com/issue-8/

"In Between." *Earth Blessings.* Edited by June Cotner. (Viva Editions, 2016): 92.

"The Skin of Your Hand." *Feminist Parenting.* Edited by Lynn Comerfield, Heather Jackson and Kandee Kasior (Demeter Press, 2016): 140.

"Let Go." voxpoetica.com 7/9/15.

"Fruit." voxpoetica.com 6/12/15.

"Dreamwaves." voxpoetica.com 5/13/15.

"The Sign." voxpoetica.com 4/15/15.

"Begun in Love." The Mom Egg Vol. 12 2014. 47-48.

"Blossom." August Avenue. April 13, 2013. http://mariascala.blogspot.com/2013/04/featured-national-poetry-month.html

"Spring Equinox, Sunday Morning." *Cyclamens and Swords.* December 2012. http://www.cyclamensandswords.com/poetry_december_2012_1.php

"Sonnet for My Daughter at 9." *Women Write Resistance: Poets Resist Gender Violence.* Edited by Laura Madeline Wiseman (Hyacinth Girl Press, 2013): 174.

"On the question of Jonah, whales, and the weight of a woman." Goblin Fruit. Summer 2012. http://www.goblinfruit.net/2012/summer/poems/?poem=jonah

"The Rock Speaks." EarthSpeak Magazine Issue 3, Spring 2010. www.earthspeakmagazine.com

"What Happens Outside When the Poets Read." EarthSpeak Magazine Issue 3, Spring 2010. www.earthspeakmagazine.com

"Calling It Down." Eclectic Flash, Volume 1. January 2010. www.eclecticflash.com Also featured as audio recording at http://www.eclecticflash.com/files/Calling_It_Down_by_Cassie_Premo_Steele.mp3

"In the Hospital at White Sands." *Martin Luther King, Jr.: An Anthology of Multicultural Poetry.* Edited by Abdul-Rasheed Na'Allah. (2009): 121.

"Bunk Bed in the Holocaust Museum." *Martin Luther King, Jr.: An Anthology of Multicultural Poetry.* Edited by Abdul-Rasheed Na'Allah. 2009): 157.

"What the Tree Has Seen." Contributors' Series 1: 9/11. November 23, 2009. www.VoxPoetica.com Reprinted in *From 9/11 to a New Year*. Edited by Annmarie Lockhart. (Unbound Content, 2010): 22-23.

"Morning Glories in Alabama." *Southern Mist*. Edited by Tom Davis. (Fayetteville, NC: Old Mountain Press, 2008): 75.

"Light My Way," *Pocket Prayers*. Edited by June Cotner. Chronicle Books, 2006. Also featured in One Spirit Book Club's mailing for May, 2006.

"Facing." *Apostrophe* (2004): 16.

"Desire." *Apostrophe* (2004): 15.

"Late January." *Blessed Bee* 19 (Winter 2003-2004): 21.

"Freya." *Earth's Daughters* #64 (2003): 26-27.

"Yemaya." *The Pagan's Muse: Poems of Ritual and Inspiration*. Edited by Jane Raeburn. (New York: Citadel Press, 2003): 12-13.

"Return." *Blessed Bee* (Spring 2003): 25.

"Lakshmi." *Aquarian Times*. (Spring 2003): 43. Reprinted in *The Pagan's Muse: Poems of Ritual and Inspiration*. Edited by Jane Raeburn. (New York: Citadel Press, 2003): 7.

"Walking the Boundary." *Savannah Literary Review* (Spring 2001): 4.

"Green is the color where winter dreams." *Savannah Literary Review* (Spring 2001): 3.

"Gaia." *AveNews*. (April/May 2001): 3.

"Dos Marias." *Knowing Stones: Poems of Exotic Places*. Edited by Maureen Tolman Flannery. (John Gordon Burke Publisher, 2000): 156.

"Each Day." *The Blessed Bee* 6 (Autumn 2000): 23.

"What the mother means to say." *The Blessed Bee* 4 (Spring 2000): 27.

"Wild." *The Blessed Bee* 3 (Winter 1999): 25.

"To Soldiers." *Out of Line* (Spring/Summer 2000): 12.

"The dust rises from the land." *MM Review* 1 (1998): 20.

"Shekhina." *2000: Here's to Humanity*. Edited by Shirley Richburg. (Baltimore, MD: The People's Press, 2000): 8.

"Artemis." *The Blessed Bee* 3 (Winter 1999): 10.

"Ishtar." *AveNews* (December 1999/January 2000): 12.

"Kore." *American Writing: A Magazine* 17 (1999): 32-33.

"Pandora." *MM Review* 1 (1998): 21.

"Asherah." *Yemassee* 5:2 (Winter/Spring 1998): 30.

"America, my mother." *The Paterson Literary Review* 27 (1997): 152.

"Field Trip to the Art Museum." *The Paterson Literary Review* 27 (1997): 153. Reprinted in Obsidian II: Black Literature in Review 12: 1-2 (1997): 71-72.

"Your voice, father." *The New Review* 4 (1997): 45.

"Witches at My Party." *The New Review* 4 (1997): 47.

"Tending." *The New Review* 4 (1997): 48.

"Come two women." *The New Review* 4 (1997): 49.

"Healing." *The New Review* 4 (1997): 51.

"To Have Been Left." *The New Review* 4 (1997): 50.

"You write what you cannot say." *The New Review* 4 (1997): 52.

"In the House of the Sun." *Messages From The Heart* 5:3(Fall 1997): 19. Reprinted in *Get Well Wishes*. Edited by June Cotner (San Francisco: HarperSanFrancisco, 2000): 74.

"Guadalupe." *Genre: An International Journal of Literature and the Arts*. Love & Power: Worlds of Dissonance and Harmony. 17 (1996): 117-120. Reprinted in *Mattoid: A Journal of Literary and Cultural Studies*. Special Issue on Crossing Cultures. Edited by Jonathan Hart. 52/53 (1998): 80-83.

"Laura's Song." *The Carolina Quarterly* 48:3 (Summer 1996): 39.

"Antidote for Witches." *The Carolina Quarterly* 48:3 (Summer 1996): 40.

"Well." *Women and Language* 17. 1 (Spring 1994): 24.

About the Author

Cassie Premo Steele is an award-winning poet and the author of 15 books of poetry, fiction, and non-fiction. She specializes in ecofeminist themes, and her writing allows for new understandings of the connections between the human and natural worlds. Her website is www.cassiepremosteele.com

Other Titles by Cassie Premo Steele

Poetry
Ruin
This is how honey runs
The Pomegranate Papers
Wednesday
Beautiful Waters

Fiction
Shamrock and Lotus

Non-fiction
We Heal from Memory
My Peace
Easyhard
Earth Joy Writing

Anthology
Moon Days

Audio
This is how honey runs
The Pomegranate Songs
Shamrock and Lotus

Selected Titles Published by Unbound Content

www.ingramcontent.com/pod-product-compliance
Lightning Source LLC
Chambersburg PA
CBHW071349090426
42738CB00012B/3063